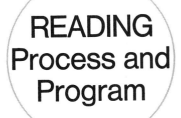

READING
Process and
Program

By Kenneth S. Goodman, *Wayne State University* &
Olive S. Niles, *Springfield Public Schools, Massachusetts*

88.352

READING
Process and
Program

COMMISSION ON THE ENGLISH CURRICULUM
NATIONAL COUNCIL OF TEACHERS OF ENGLISH

CONSULTANT READERS FOR THIS MANUSCRIPT/
ROBERT FARRAR KINDER, State Department of Education,
Hartford, Connecticut · WALTER J. MOORE, University of
Illinois · COMMITTEE ON PUBLICATIONS/ ROBERT F.
HOGAN, NCTE Executive Secretary, Chairman · ROBERT
DYKSTRA, University of Minnesota · WALKER GIBSON,
University of Massachusetts · MILDRED E. WEBSTER, St.
Joseph Senior High School, Michigan · EUGENE C. ROSS,
NCTE Director of Publications

EDITORIAL SERVICES/ Diane H. Allen, NCTE Headquarters

BOOK DESIGN/ Norma Phillips Meyers, NCTE Headquarters

Library of Congress Catalog Card Number: 77-139591
Standard Book Number: 8141-5095-5
NCTE Stock Number: 50955

Contents

READING
Process and
Program

Foreword

In 1966, the Commission on the English Curriculum began an intended series of short monographs on curriculum issues and trends in teaching the English language arts. The first monograph, under the general editorship of Alexander Frazier, was titled *Ends and Issues—1965-1966*. Rather than attempt to answer the many questions which surround and recur in the English language arts, this volume sought to systematize the questions, to pose them in a framework of current scholarship on the many facets of the discipline, and to suggest that the questions posed in the booklet be asked by any group seeking to develop its own curriculum outlines.

A notable omission in the booklet was the topic of reading, particularly that aspect of reading lying close to basic skills and initial instruction in reading. The causes for omission were multiple, chief among them being time and the size of the Commission's task in getting *Ends and Issues* into the hands of teachers faced with curriculum decisions in a time of change. But still the omission troubled the Commission, for no work pretending to broach and encompass the English language arts can be complete without accounting for critically important questions about reading.

The delay in accounting for reading was fortuitous, for it allowed the Commission time to settle upon the right persons to bring forth a companion monograph on reading which would round out *Ends and Issues.* Under the leadership of Director Robert Bennett, the Commission on the English Curriculum commissioned Kenneth S. Goodman of Wayne State University and Olive S. Niles of the Springfield, Massachusetts, Public Schools to write the present monograph. Commission members Harold Herber and Robert B. Ruddell worked closely with the authors during preparation of the manuscript.

The title of this monograph may seem presumptuous at first glance; and one might explain the presumption by stating that the titling seeks only to compensate for the incomplete fulfillment of *Ends and Issues.* But, in a real sense, the title is apt; for the authors have dealt with broad and major concerns in reading, accounted for insights from related fields, set forth a provocative conception of reading as a psycholinguistic process, described the conditions necessary for effective reading instruction in secondary schools, and described current trends in reading instruction. In contrast with *Ends and Issues,* the present publication does not present a series of questions to be pondered by curriculum makers; rather, the authors set forth positions to be discussed, examined and tested by both researchers and practitioners.

In Part 1, Goodman describes reading within a transformational-generative framework, as essentially a set of processes of recoding, decoding and encoding leading ultimately to comprehension, in his view the only real objective of reading. Comprehension, he points out, is not a necessarily transferable skill, and encounters between the pupil and special types of writing such as literature, textbook prose, and reading in special content fields pose specific reading problems which must be met specifically. For pupils who come from culturally different backgrounds, our assumptions about experience and vocabulary pose additional problems, Goodman asserts—problems not only for the pupil, but also for the schools which select the reading materials to be used for such children.

Perhaps the most provocative aspect of the monograph is Goodman's model of the reading process, a model which attempts to account for all the multiple behaviors which appear to be evident in reading—the starting, the checking, the comparing with known alternatives, the recycling and, where possible, the comprehension and storing of informational data when success is achieved. The total effect suggests that the human reader—even the young reader—is performing with a complexity that we often fail to appreciate.

Throughout the monograph, there is expressed a profound respect for the linguistic competence of children with spoken language, a resource which we do not yet know how to tap in order to produce a similar competence in reading, particularly for the minority of children whom we cannot seem to reach through present programs. But, despite the problems of learning to read and read well, Goodman sees hope that we may be verging on a new era in reading—that this decade may be the one in which the major problems in reading can be solved.

In Part 2, Niles leads us to consider the total framework for a secondary school reading program—the climate for reading instruction, the modes of school and class organization useful for effective reading instruction, some promising trends in reading instruction, the selection and preparation of teachers of reading, the inservice improvement of reading instruction, and improvements needed in reading materials and their use. Niles concludes with a glance toward the near future when improved modes of curriculum construction, improved technology, and improved conditions for teaching reading augur well for children and youth.

The Commission on the English Curriculum is indebted to the authors for the incisiveness and range of their thinking, the provocativeness of their suggestions and the clarity of their writing which we believe will do much to generate thoughtful discussions about reading in the months and years to come.

The Commission on the English Curriculum welcomes the formation of an NCTE Commission on Reading under the leadership of Robert B. Ruddell of the University of California,

Berkeley. Though the Commission on Curriculum does not intend to abandon its concern about reading, it does recognize that reading is a critical aspect of the language arts and requires and deserves the special attention that the new commission will give to it in coming years. We hope that somehow this present monograph will help make the work of the new commission fruitful.

John C. Maxwell, Director
Commission on the English Curriculum

BEHIND THE EYE:
What Happens in Reading

A child, eyebrows knit, haltingly speaks as he stares intently at the small book he is holding, "See Tom. See Tom . . ." He stops, apparently unable to continue. "We haven't had that next word yet," he states in a troubled voice to his teacher.

"Mary is only seven, but she can read anything," says the doting mother to her friend. "Read us that article from the *Times*," she says to the little girl. The child reads an article on national politics, with great speed and animation, while the friend listens appreciatively. She stumbles occasionally, as the going gets rough now and then, but is apparently untroubled by the task. "Did you understand all that dear?" her awed listener asks. "She has a little difficulty putting it into words, but I'm sure she understands," interposes the mother.

"I give up," the weary graduate student mutters to himself as he sits at the small table in the library stacks. He's just finished his third reading of the article his professor has assigned. He forces himself to formulate, out of the conceptual jumble he finds himself lost in, a few questions to raise in class. "Maybe the class is too advanced for me," he wonders. "Why don't these guys write so people can understand?"

"I can't make head or tail out of this damn thing." A best-selling writer is speaking long-distance to his attorney. "It's some kind of release I'm supposed to sign giving this producer the film rights to my latest book. But it's full of all kinds of parties of the first part and whereas's."

"Read it to me," says the lawyer. The author begins. "The undersigned, who shall be known as . . ." The attorney listens, interrupts a few times to ask for repetition, and is ready by the time his caller has finished to offer his legal advice. He clarifies the meaning of the document to the author, restates the legal terminology in phrases his client finds meaningful, dictates a clause to be added to protect the author's rights.

Reading is obviously involved in each of these episodes. But, at what point does it become reading and at what point does it cease to be reading and become something else, thinking perhaps, or concept formation, or the acquisition of knowledge?

Is the child who is limited to calling the names of word shapes he has been taught in any sense a reader? If he is not, at what point does he become one? Is it when he has a larger sight-word repertoire? How large? Is it when he has learned how to "attack" new words? If, like the hypothetical Mary above, he can "read" things he can't understand, is he reading?

To what extent must a reader arrive at the meaning the writer intended? If he must fully *comprehend,* then our graduate student is a non-reader. Even if a moderate level of comprehension is required he has fallen short of the mark. Are all readers then only semiliterate?

Who has read the legal document? The lawyer who is hundreds of miles away from it and who cannot even see it, or his client who holds it in his hand? Or did reading require both of their contributions? Shall we call what the author did reading, and his attorney's contribution interpretation? Or shall we say that the author was word-calling and the lawyer comprehending?

The issues which are raised in these episodes are neither simple nor easily answered. To a certain extent, of course, we can be arbitrary. We can define reading to be anything we choose. But if our definition is to be useful, it must be one we can use consistently; it must be inclusive of that which is relevant and exclusive of that which is not. It must also be productive. Definitions which are too narrow or too broad or too vague or too specific tend to cut off or dissipate inquiry rather than promote it. Further, a definition must be consistent with reality.

To move us toward a definition of reading, it may help to list certain evident aspects of the process:

- Reading begins with graphic language in some form: print, script, etc.
- The purpose of reading is the reconstruction of meaning. Meaning is not in print, but it is meaning that the author begins with when he writes. Somehow the reader strives to *reconstruct* this meaning as he reads.
- In alphabetic writing systems there is a direct relationship between oral language and written language.
- Visual perception must be involved in reading.
- Nothing intrinsic in the writing system or its symbols has meaning. There is nothing in the shape or sequence of any letters or grouping of letters which in itself is meaning.
- Meaning is in the mind of the writer and the mind of the reader.
- Yet readers are capable through reading of reconstructing a message which agrees with the writer's intended message.

A Definition of Reading

At this point, we're ready to state a definition of reading: *Reading is a complex process by which a reader reconstructs, to some degree, a message encoded by a writer in graphic language.*

In this definition it is no more significant that the reader starts with graphic input [1] than that he ends with meaning. To understand this process, we must understand the nature of the graphic input. We must understand how language works and how language is used by the reader. We must understand how much meaning depends on the reader's prior learning and experience in the reconstruction of meaning. We must understand the perceptual system involved in reading. As we come to see the reader as a user of language, we will understand that reading is a psycholinguistic process, an interaction between thought and language.

Written Language: The Nature of the Graphic Input

Written English is, of course, an alphabetic system. It uses a set of letters almost directly adapted from the Latin. The Latin alphabet in turn was derived from the Greek. Most modern languages are written with alphabets derived from the same group of ancient, related alphabets. Alphabetic writing differs from other systems in that the system is a representation not of meaning directly, but of oral language. In original intent, the units of written language (letters) represented the sound units of speech rather than meanings as in pictographic and other systems.

Oral language is produced in a time sequence, but written language must be arranged spatially. Though various arrangements are possible, and used in other systems, in English print is arranged from left to right and top to bottom in successive lines. White space separates patterns of letters just as oral patterns are marked by intonation contours, pauses, pitch sequences, and relative stressing. Larger patterns require markings, punctuation, to set them off from other patterns. Again, intonational features are replaced to some degree in print by periods, commas, and other graphic signals. In this feature, as in a number

---

[1] As we think of reading as an information seeking process, it will help to think of the graphic material as input and meaning as output. Oral reading produces speech as a second output.

of others, there is no one-to-one correspondence between oral and written language. The intonation pattern of a question like "Do you understand?" is distributed over the whole oral sentence, while graphically it is represented only by a capital letter at the beginning and a question mark at the end. It is marked as different from the statement form only at the end. (Contrast Spanish which puts a question mark at both ends.)

Relationships between Oral and Written English

While written language is a secondary form, both historically and in the personal history of any individual, it must be seen as a different but parallel form to oral language, since both for the literate user are fully capable of meeting the complex needs of communication. Written language has the advantage, only recently made possible for oral language, of being perfectable and preservable. Oral language on the other hand is more easily and more rapidly produced in a wider range of circumstances.

Having said that English uses an alphabetic writing system, we must now caution that the set of relationships between oral and written English is not a simple small set of letter-to-sound correspondences (or phoneme-to-grapheme ones, to use linguistic terms). For several reasons, to be accurate, we must say that the relationships are between patterns of sounds and patterns of letters. The most significant of these reasons is that spelling patterns are basically standard and stable while oral language changes over time and space.

Spellings are standard. Standard spellings were developed by printers in the early years of the development of printing and the spread of literacy. Though Americans may differ from the British in the spellings of a very few words like "labor" (labour), there is great agreement on word spellings among speakers of all English dialects. *Pumpkin* is the spelling whether one says *punkin, ponkin, pumpkin* or whatever. This is, of course, a considerable advantage, since written communication between speakers of diverse English dialects is made more effective. Any other arrangement would require establishment of a standard dialect upon which to base spelling. Subsequently either the dialect would need to be protected from change or periodical updating of the spelling system to catch up with the changes would be required. If this could be accomplished, the spelling system would be highly suited for the one dialect's speakers, but increasingly dysfunctional for all others. Change is always going on in language. It cannot in any case be closed off. No lesser man than Napoleon tried and failed to keep language from changing.

Oral language sequences. Another factor in making the relationships between oral and written English complex has to do with the nature of oral language sound sequences. For example, note these related words: *site, situate,* and *situation.* In *site,* we have a well known pattern with a vowel-consonant-e. (V-C-e) The *e* serves as a pattern marker. Notice that the relationship of the prior vowel to a sound is not clear without the rest of the spelling pattern. But when, through affixes, the word *situate* is formed, a sound sequence occurs after the /t/ which requires a shift in the oral form to a *ch* sound /č/. The same shift occurs in the word sequence *don't you.* We must either change the spelling to *ch* or retain the *t* and lose the close letter-sound correspondence. Similar shifting is required in moving to *situation* where the sound becomes *sh* /š/. The spelling system has alternatives. It may retain the close correspondence of sounds and letters and thus change spellings as the sounds shift. Or it may retain the letters even when the sound shifts and thus preserve the derivational character of the word relationships. The system tends to do the latter perhaps because speakers of the language seem to shift as required so automatically that they are not bothered by the spelling discrepancy. It simply sounds too strange to his ears for a speaker of English to say *situation* differently. This may be illustrated with this nonsense word offered in three alternate spellings: *boft, boffed, bofd.* The final consonant cluster is pronounced the same by native speakers of

English. Because /f/ precedes the final consonant, the latter is produced as /t/; spelling cannot induce a speaker to abandon that pronunciation.

Much has been written about regular and irregular relationships between oral and written English. The distinction loses its meaning if we understand that the patterns of correspondence are complex, but systematic. Some examples above have already illustrated this complex-regularity. Here is another: *s* may not frequently represent the sound *sh* /š/, but when it does, as in *sure* and *sugar,* the circumstances are consistent ones and it is thus every bit as regular in its representation as it is in *sister. Hymn, damn, bomb, sign,* appear irregularly spelled, but they are not so if we consider the "silent letters" relate to derived forms such as *hymnal, damnation, bombard, signal.*

A number of early applications to reading materials which stressed linguistics tended to apply a rather narrow view of regular letter-sound correspondence. The Bloomfield-Barnhart materials, the SRA Linguistic Readers, and the Harper-Row Linguistic Science Readers are examples. The Merrill Linguistic Readers, based on the work of C. C. Fries, had a somewhat broader view of regularity as represented in spelling patterns.

The Nature of Language

If we are to define and understand reading, we must understand the nature of language itself. Paradoxically, language is learned so early and so well that we tend to take its functioning for granted.

How Language Works

Language is always a means and only rarely an end in itself. We are so distracted, as we use it, by meaning (the end for which language is the means), that we are quite unaware of how language works to convey meaning. Consider, for example, a simple statement: *John hit Bill.* In either oral or written form, it is not the symbols, phonemes, or letters but the systematic structuring of these symbols that makes comprehension of meaning possible.

The listener or reader must recognize the patterns *John, hit,* and *Bill* and he must also recognize the pattern of patterns which makes a statement of relationships possible. The difference between *John hit Bill* and *Bill hit John* is in the sentence patterns or syntax. Nothing else tells the listener or reader whether Bill or John hit John or Bill. Grammar, the system of language, makes it possible for language to convey the most complex relationships humans conceive.

All language is patterned: the patterns are the sequences in which the elements may occur. In *John hit Bill,* it is pattern alone which tells the listener who was hitting and who was being hit.

In English, pattern is itself the single most important aspect of grammar. Other languages make more use of word changes (inflections) such as affixes to carry extensive portions of the grammatical system. In such languages the nominative and accusative endings might have differentiated the aggressor from the victim in the example above. English preserves such a system in its pronouns. *I hit him* and *He hit me* use different forms in grammatical cases. But notice that we still would not say *Him hit I.* Pattern is still preserved.

Certain English words and word parts serve as pattern markers. In a statement like *A man was feeding his dogs,* we have a pattern: A ——— was ———ing his ———s. The pattern markers, function words like *A, his,* and *was,* and inflectional endings like *ing,* and *s* set the pattern up. In themselves none of these elements carry meaning. But without the grammatical pattern they create, we cannot express even the simplest relationship between the words that do carry meaning.

How Language Is Used

When a child undertakes to learn to read at the age of five or six, he is already a skilled user of language. He has somehow learned to generate language to communicate his thoughts, emotions, and needs to his family and peers. Further, he is able to comprehend what other people say to him. To state that he has learned by imitation does not accurately represent the case. He has, in fact, devised language for himself which moves toward the norms of adult language because the more it does, the more effective he is in communication.

Moreover, he has not simply acquired a collection of words or sentences to use when the occasion is appropriate. He has learned the rules by which language is produced. Language is rule-governed. As long as a child can only produce language he has already heard, his language capability is severely limited. Infinite numbers of sentences are possible in a language. If a child had to hear them and learn them before he could use them, language learning would be a much slower process than it is. But a small number of rules govern language production. These are the rules that tell the child which noun to put before and which after a transitive verb when he runs up to a teacher on the playground and says, "John hit Bill." They are the rules that make it possible for him to say, "When I hit him, he hits me back," getting *hit* and *hits* in the right position and making one clause subordinate to another. They are the rules that make it possible for him to say things he has never heard anyone say before and be sure that other speakers of the language will understand.

Generating Language. In speaking or in writing, meaning in the mind of the originator creates a deep language structure (a set of base forms) and activates a set of rules which transform that structure and generate a signal, either graphic or oral. This process must be a complete one. The signal must have a surface structure which is complete. All essential elements must be present, and extraneous ones must not be. We might describe this whole process as *encoding*. A structured code signal has been produced. The user of a language has so well learned this encoding procedure that it is virtually automatic. Meaning, as a language user formulates it, literally creates an automatic chain of events which results in language code. A model of speech, quite simplified, is reprinted in Figure 1 on the following page.

FIGURE 1
Spoken Language

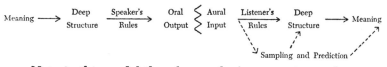

Note in this model that the speaker's output is not the same as the listener's input. What is said is not precisely what is heard, just as in reading what is written is not precisely what is read. This relationship might be compared to the relationship of fetus and mother. Her bloodstream nourishes the uterine wall from which the fetus draws its nourishment, through its own bloodstream. But, the two bloodstreams are not connected.

Note also that meaning is not in the oral output or the aural input. Meaning is only in the minds of the speaker and the listener. The listener (like the reader) must recreate meaning for himself from the input he has obtained.

Language has been learned by the listener in the context of experience as it was used in those situations by people around him. His ability to recreate meaning depends on his ability to associate those experiences and the concepts he has formed through them with the language.

The speaker in generating language must produce a sound sequence which is decodable by the listener. In this oral language signal, the sounds must be sufficiently well articulated and the structure sufficiently complete that the listener has all the information he needs.

At first appearances, it would seem that listening would be a kind of mirror image of speech with the process simply reversed to get from surface structure of aural language to meaning.

In fact, however, the listener may, through a process that combines sampling and prediction, leap to the deep structure and meaning without using all the information available to him. He acquires strategies as a language user that enable him to select only the most productive cues. His user's knowledge of language structure and the redundancy [2] of that structure make it possible for him to predict and anticipate the grammatical pattern on the basis of identifying a few elements in it. The context in which the language occurs, created by the previous meanings he has gathered, allows him to predict the meaning of what will follow. All these combine to make listening related to but a very different process from speaking.

Perception in Listening and Reading

Before we compare listening and reading, let's explore how perception operates in listening. Every language uses a small number of sound units, which some linguists label phonemes. These are in reality bundles of sounds which are treated by listeners as the same. Just as we call many different colors and shades of colors red, we hear many different sounds as /t/. Two colors could be quite similar, but one would be called red and the other orange, while two other more dissimilar colors might be both called red. In the same way the *phoneme* is a perceptual category. As a language is learned these categories become functional. The child learns to treat certain differences as significant and others as insignificant. *In short, he not only learns what to pay attention to, but, equally important, what not to pay attention to.* So the native speaker of Japanese learning English does not distinguish *late* from *rate* because he has learned to ignore a difference which isn't significant in Japanese. Similarly, a speaker of English has difficulty differentiating the Spanish *pero* (but) from *perro* (dog).[3]

Perception in language is and must be both selective and anticipatory. To be aware of what is significant in language one

---

[2] Redundancy means, here, that each bit of information may be conveyed by several cues in the language. For example, notice in this sentence how many cues indicate the plural nature of the subject: *Two boys are eating their sandwiches.*

[3] If you don't hear the difference, then you don't know Spanish phonemes, which is the point here.

must ignore what is not. Perception, to be functional in listening, must be augmented by anticipation. The sounds are so fleeting and follow each other so rapidly that time does not allow for each to be fully perceived and identified. Mastery of the phonological system, however, and of the grammatical system as well, enables the listener to use partial perceptions and sample the input. Under some circumstances, of course, the partial perceptions may be too fragmentary or distorted and the listener may have to ask for repetition. But, to be quite blunt, what we think we hear is as much what we expect to hear as it is what we do hear.

Contrast the task of repeating even a short sequence in a foreign language with a comparable or longer one in a known language. The foreign language simply doesn't correspond to available perceptual categories, nor can we fit what we do catch into any system that would aid prediction.

Perception in language use cannot be viewed then as a simple series of sound perceptions or word perceptions. It must be understood in relation to the grammatical structure of the language, and to the structure of the meaning which is being communicated.

All that has been said in comparing speaking and listening basically applies to the parallel language processes, writing and reading.

The writer generates his signal in exactly the same way that the speaker does. In the last stage, these generative processes differ. In speech, a series of phonological rules determines the exact sound sequences which will be uttered. In writing, instead of phonological rules a set of graphotactic rules (spelling if you prefer) produces the exact grapheme sequences.

As we have indicated earlier, though both speaking and writing must produce complete signals, writing is usually polished and perfected to a greater degree than speech through editing by the author. Furthermore, the reader works from a more or less permanent graphic input while the listener must contend with input that in most cases perishes as it is produced.

Rereading is possible. Relistening requires that the speaker cooperate in repeating what he has said.

But reading, like listening, is a sampling, predicting, guessing process. Proficient readers, in fact, learn to use the reading process much more rapidly than they normally use the listening process. Listening is held pretty much to the rate at which speech is produced. That, of course, is much slower than the processing of average proficient readers.

In the guessing game which is reading, three types of information are used. Each has several subtypes. They are used in reading simultaneously and not sequentially.

Information Used during the Reading Process

I. Grapho-phonic Information
   A. Graphic Information: The letters, spelling patterns and patterns of patterns created through white space and punctuation. A word or suffix represents a graphic pattern; a phrase or sentence is a pattern of patterns.
   B. Phonological Information: The sounds, sound patterns and patterns of patterns created through intonation (pitch, stress, pause). Read any line on this page and note how these work.
   C. Phonic Information: The complex set of relationships between the graphic and phonological representations of the language. Notice here we are speaking of the relationships and not an instructional program for teaching them.

II. Syntactic Information
   A. Sentence Patterns: The grammatical sequences and inter-relationships of language. The ——s ——ed the ——s, is an example of a sentence pattern common in English.
   B. Pattern Markers: The markers which outline the patterns.
      1. Function Words: Those very frequent words which, though themselves relatively without definable mean-

ing, signal the grammatical function of the other elements. Examples: *the, was, not, do, in, very, why, but.*

2. Inflections: Those bound morphemes (affixes) which convey basically grammatical information. Examples: *ing, ed, s.*

3. Punctuation — Intonation: The system of markings and space distribution and the related intonation patterns. Pitch and stress variations and variable pauses in speech are represented to some extent by punctuation in writing.

C. Transformational Rules: These are not characteristic of the graphic input itself, but are supplied by the reader in response to what he perceives as its surface structure. They carry him to the deep structure and meaning. If he is to recognize and derive meaning from a graphic pattern, he must bring these grammatical rules into the process.

III. Semantic Information

A. Experience: The reader brings *his* prior experiences into play in response to the graphic input.

B. Concepts: The reader organizes the meaning he is reconstructing according to his existing concepts and reorganizes experience into concepts as he reads.

C. Vocabulary is largely a term for the ability of the child to sort out his experiences and concepts in relation to words and phrases in the context of what he is reading.

All of these kinds of information are available to the reader at the same time in graphic language. In the sampling process, they support each other much as they do in listening. Particular cues take on strategic importance in relation to the full array of information in the input which they could not have in isolation. In a list a word like *the,* for example, is a word with little or no referential meaning. It summons forth, from the reader's stockpile of information, no experiences or concepts. But put *the* into a sentence and it becomes a grammatical cue of some importance. In these sequences: *He hurried to farm* (his land) and *he hurried to the farm, farm* is marked as a noun in the second sequence by *the*, whereas in the first, *farm* is a verb and the reader will expect an object to follow.

The relationship between oral and written language is of more significance in reading than in listening. Particularly in learning to read the language he speaks, a child may draw on his oral language competence as he develops control over written language. The alphabetic character of the writing system makes it possible to match sound sequences already known with less familiar graphic sequences.

A possible simplified model for reading in early stages might look like this:

FIGURE 2

EARLY READING [4]

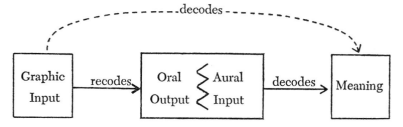

The child here recodes graphic input as speech (either out-loud or internally) and then, utilizing his own speech as aural input, decodes as he does in listening. Notice the model assumes some direct decoding from print to meaning, even at early stages.

---

[4] In this diagram, *recode* is used to mean going from code to code (aural to graphic); *decode* is reserved for processes that go from code (in either form) to meaning. In this sense, comprehension and *decoding* are virtual synonyms while word-calling and sounding-out are *recoding* processes. A third term, *encode*, is used to mean going from meaning to code (again either written or oral). In our early example of the writer and his attorney, the writer could only *recode* printed language as oral language. But the lawyer could *decode* from language to meaning. Then he could *encode* meaning in an oral language form his client could *decode* (comprehend).

Some writers on the topic of reading have assumed that for instructional purposes these two aspects, recoding and decoding, are separable. And indeed, materials and methods have been built on that assumption. As a prereading program, instruction is provided to the child in matching letters and sounds (i.e., synthetic phonics, Sullivan's programed reading) or in matching spelling patterns and sound patterns (e.g., Fries Linguistic Readers) or in matching oral names with graphic shapes (sight vocabulary). But in all of these types of recoding instruction, the reader is confined to words or word parts and may not sample the syntactic or semantic information that would be available in full language. What's more, the process is one in which meaning cannot result. Thus by our tentative definition, (see p. 5) recoding in itself is not reading.

In any case, a second instructional phase would be needed to help the learner adapt his recoding strategies and techniques to the full language situation in which all information is available and decoding may result.

Reading does eventually become a parallel process to listening which then would have this appearance:

FIGURE 3

PROFICIENT READING

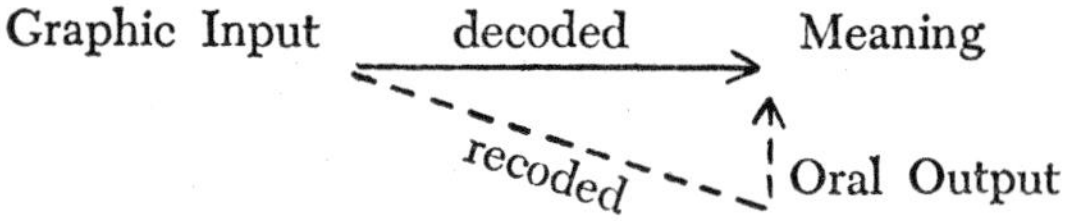

In this model, recoding has at best a supplementary role. The basic decoding is directly from print to meaning, though there is some echo of speech involved as the reader proceeds even in silent reading. At times, the reader may find it helpful to recode print as speech and then decode. (The reverse may also be true for literate speakers. They may occasionally "write it down," recoding speech as graphic input and then decoding.)

When silent reading becomes proficient, it becomes a very different process from oral reading. It is much more rapid and not tied to encoding what is being read as speech. In silent reading, the reader sweeps ahead sampling from the graphic input, predicting structures, leaping to quick conclusions about the meaning and only slowing down or regressing when subsequent sampling fails to confirm what he expects to find.

Oral reading which is fluent and accurate may involve simultaneous recoding and decoding. But for most proficient silent readers, who don't have much occasion for oral reading, oral reading apparently follows this model:

FIGURE 4

ORAL READING

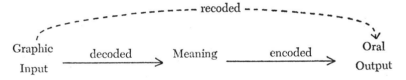

Primarily oral output is produced *after* meaning has been decoded and hence, though comprehension may be high, the oral output is often a poor match for the graphic input. The reader sounds clumsy and makes numerous errors.

The diagram on pages 30 and 31 illustrates in some detail the psycholinguistic process which is silent reading. This model represents the *proficient* reader, but it also represents the competence which is the goal of reading instruction.

Reading is an active process in which the reader selects the fewest cues possible from those available to him and makes the best choices possible. If he is highly proficient, he will have good speed and high comprehension; reading will be a smooth process. If he is less proficient or if he is encountering unusually difficult material (as in the case of the graduate student in our early examples), reading will be less smooth and will involve considerable cycling back to gather more cues and make better choices.

Meaning is the constant goal of the proficient reader and he continually tests his choices against the developing meaning by asking himself if what he is reading makes sense. The process does not require that he perceive and identify every cue. In fact that would be both unnecessary and inefficient. But it does require that the reader monitor his choices so he can recognize his errors and gather more cues when needed.

Such traditional terms as *word recognition, sounding out,* and *word attack* stem from a view of reading as a succession of accurate perceptions or word identifications. Such a view is not consistent with the actual performance of proficient readers.

The Application of Reading

Reading, if it is sucessful, is, as we have shown, not a passive process. The reader is a language user who interacts with the graphic input. Successful reading yields meaning which becomes the means to further ends. The reader may follow directions, respond to questions, read further. The extent and direction of application depend on the nature and purpose of what is read. Literary materials, because of their aesthetic, stylistic qualities, yield a kind of pleasure and satisfaction which creates further appetite for literature. Plot and story line in literature propel the reader forward. "I just couldn't put it down," he may say.

Informational materials may have a similar effect; new knowledge leads to a desire for more knowledge. Or such material may meet a small but immediate need, as for example when the reader needs to clarify a particular fact in the encyclopedia.

Language and thought are interactive in reading, but at some point thought processes leap out and away from the message of the writer.

In this interaction a reader may be involved in cycles of reading, reflective thinking, flights of fancy and then more reading. In certain kinds of materials, recipes for example, the reader may follow a *read* and *do* cycle. He reads and then gathers his ingredients; then he reads again and performs step one and so forth.

Though reading and the application of the fruits of reading are separable, it must always be remembered that reading is never pursued for its own sake, even in literature. If the reader finds no "payoff," he will not continue to read. This is as true in the stages in which reading is being acquired as it is in the stages of proficient reading.

Materials used in the teaching of reading at all stages must necessarily be meaningful. Children with different purposes and interests will need a variety of materials to keep them reading. Ironically, development of reading competence is best achieved when the learner's focus is on the content of materials and not on reading itself. Social studies, science, mathematics, literature and other materials contribute well to the child's reading development while serving other curricular ends, if their conceptual load is not too heavy.

Adaptation in Reading

By the time he undertakes to become literate in his native language every child has acquired considerable competence [5] in its basic communicative use. The basic form of his language, that used in common discourse and conversation, is his means of communication, expression, thinking, and learning. It makes sense to start with this common discursive language in reading.

---

[5] We use *competence* here, as some linguists do, to represent the basic, developed capacity for using language. *Performance* is a behavioral indicator of that *competence* but behavior should not be confused with the abilities that make performance possible. (Further elaboration is offered on pp. 26-27.)

Experience stories, directions, labels, signs are examples of early reading materials that use common language.

Children have not necessarily acquired the same kind of competence in dealing with other specialized forms of language. Literature utilizes one such special form. The language of literature has its own special set of rules and contingencies. Poetic license makes it possible for the poet to reverse some key language priorities for the sake of meter, rhyme, or mood. Similarly, literary prose employs structures and language devices differently from common language.

The strategies which the child has learned in listening transfer well to reading common language. To deal with literary language he will need to modify his strategies and perhaps acquire some new ones.

A good deal of prereading experience with literature will help the child build a strong base for reading literature for himself. Some children grow up in a world of literature: they are surrounded by books; their parents read to them; they acquire favorites which they soon know by heart. By the time such children come to school, they have a feel for the peculiarities of literary language and a sense of what to expect from it. They can predict in literary language as they can in more common language. For the large number of children who lack such background, teachers can begin to build it through oral reading to the children and other devices while the more basic literacy ability is being built.

Subsequently, children can begin to read literary language. As they do so, they will necessarily modify the techniques and strategies they use in reading to accommodate the structure of literary language. Even then, it will probably make the most sense to start with literary forms and themes which are most like common language and move to literary forms which deviate more. Folk and fairy tales may be pleasurable to the child because of their familiarity. But the archaic language, the unusual structure, and the allegorical nature of their plots may combine to make them unsuitable for early literature reading. One possibility, of course, is to rewrite them for young children in order to eliminate these problems. A criticism of that approach is that in the process their qualities as literature may be lost and they may become dull and lacking in color and characterization. In a similar sense, adaptations of great works of literature for children too young to handle the original may make them more readable but destroy their essential merits. In both cases, such critics conclude it might be better to postpone reading such materials until the child's reading competence has reached a point where he is ready to learn to cope with the special demands they make on him.

Research into literary style is beginning to suggest that writers employ less common language structures frequently to achieve a sense of individuality and distinction. If this is true, then some specific assistance to children in recognizing and predicting these structures may greatly enhance their ability to read particular authors.

In the past several decades, a large and varied literature especially written for children of various ages has been produced. Such literature makes it possible to guide youngsters through material which they can select to suit their own interests and levels of ability. In the process, they will build their ability to deal with more sophisticated literature. A number of publishers have organized better selections in kits with multiple copies of each title and teacher guide material.

Schools present the learners with the need for dealing with a number of other special forms of language. Textbooks, in general, use language in special ways which vary from common language use. They tend, particularly in elementary and secondary schools, to present a very large number of topics, facts, and concepts rapidly and superficially. Reading to learn may well stimulate learning to read, but only if the concept load (roughly the number of new ideas presented) is not so heavy as to cause the reader to lose any sense of meaning. *Textbook reading, through the elementary years at least, probably requires considerable introductory, preparatory work on the part of the teacher.* Concepts and ideas can be introduced through demonstration, experimentation, concrete illustration. Vocabulary can be developed orally in relationship to these experiences. Then, and only then, is the child ready for the task of reading about the same concepts in the text. He reads them not so much to gain new concepts as to reinforce them. In the process, he learns to handle the unusual language uses of textbooks. If textbooks are well written and handled well in elementary schools, he may, by the time he is in high school, be able to initiate study at times through a textbook with the teacher following up and reteaching the concepts he meets in the books.

Another alternative is to change our thinking about how textbooks are used in elementary and junior high schools. Part of the problem with textbooks is that they move rapidly from topic to topic, a fact inherent in the nature of the task they undertake. Consequently, they present a large vocabulary of terms not well developed in context. Perhaps multimedia approaches would help; kits and coordinated packages containing film loops, audio and video tapes, transparencies, and other materials as well as reading materials could replace the single text. The texts could become elements in resource kits to provide more specific focus on single concepts or depth treatment of groups of related concepts.

Children will encounter problems in learning to deal with other kinds of reference books too. The need for reference skills, use of index, contents and glossary is obvious. Less obvious problems involve strategies for dealing with specialized vocabulary and language structures. Encyclopedias, for example, employ distinctive writing styles. There are also key problems for the reader in learning to modify his whole reading style to reference reading. Even graduate students do not always have effective techniques for selecting and reading from reference works only those portions germane to their needs. Skimming is one of several gross sampling strategies needed for specific use in some kinds of reference work.

Science, mathematics, social studies, music, art, industrial arts, home economics, in fact all school subjects, require learners to handle special kinds of language. It cannot be assumed that general reading competence leads automatically to these special abilities. Using a recipe, following a set of plans, interpreting a contour map, following a laboratory procedure—all present special reading problems. The abilities required must of course be developed in the context of the tasks. To pick an example, a reader can't learn how to read a recipe unless he is really making something. And the best test of the effectiveness of the reading will be the way the final product tastes. The implication is apparent. *Every teacher of whatever subject and level must be prepared to help children to meet new demands on their reading competence and to develop the special strategies which these demands require.*[6]

A special word needs to be said about vocabulary. Every time a learner pushes into a new field or into a new subject area within an old one, he encounters new vocabulary or new uses for old terms. That problem is a by-product of his quest for knowledge. The vocabulary is unfamiliar because the ideas and concepts it expresses are unfamiliar. Like new concepts, new vocabulary learned in relationship to the new knowledge must be built on the base of pre-existing vocabulary. If the new vocabulary is more effective in manipulating the new ideas it will be absorbed, and old language may be modified or set aside. *Vocabulary development outside of the context of new ideas and pre-existing language is not possible.*

What we commonly call a vocabulary problem is never simply a matter of putting a verbal label on an object. In reality, it may represent a variety of different problems.

1. The reader encounters a printed form he does not recognize for a word in his oral vocabulary. This is the simplest vocabulary problem since he has experiences and concepts to relate to his oral vocabulary.

---

[6] Of course it will also help to assure that materials children are asked to read are written well. Poor writing is not likely to be easily read.

2. The reader encounters a printed form which is not familiar and not in his oral vocabulary. But the concept is a known one. He has other language forms to express it. In this case the problem is to associate new language with old.

3. The reader encounters a printed form which is unfamiliar, has no oral counterpart for him, and represents a concept which is new to him. He may in fact lack relevant experience on which to base such a concept. This is the case in which vocabulary must follow conceptual development. Otherwise, we have a fourth possibility.

4. A written form is familiar and may even have an oral equivalent, but the reader has no meaning for it. Within narrow limits he may even use it to answer test questions correctly without understanding what he is reading.

5. The final possibility exists as readers become proficient. They may encounter printed forms and come to attach concepts to them without ever encountering them in oral speech. One does not have to be able to pronounce a word to understand it.

Objectives of the Reading Curriculum

Once we have defined reading and discussed it as a process, a next step in considering reading curricula is to restate this process as a series of objectives. First, however, an important distinction must be made. That is the distinction between language competence and language performance.

Competence and Performance

Much has been said in curricular literature about behavioral objectives. In this view, the ultimate objective of instruction is always to change behavior (which we treat as a synonym for performance). But this view fails to take into account the concept that there is underlying all performance a basic competence.

It is this underlying competence, and not the behavior itself, which we seek to build through education.

Above we delineated some variations involved in vocabulary. To use this as an example, in expanding vocabulary we must not mistake performance, the uttering of words, for competence, the understanding which must underlie the effective use of words. Too often school lessons change performance (behavior) but only superficially get at competence, and thus a change is a temporary or meaningless one.

While we must seek evidence in performance of the competence which learners have achieved, we must be very cautious of either equating performance and competence or of interpreting performance too directly and simplistically.

In language and reading this distinction is particularly important. Vocabulary, to continue the example, is going to develop in direct ratio to the experience and interest that a learner has. *Low vocabulary yield in the performance of children in certain task situations cannot be directly interpreted to mean that the child has a small vocabulary.* It may mean only that the topic or topics were not ones which interested him; it might also mean that for various reasons such as fear, unfamiliarity of the situation or the interviewers, or disdain for the task or teacher, the child simply did not perform in any way representative of his competence.

Here is another example: There are periods in the development of reading competence when oral reading becomes very awkward.[7] Readers who have recently become rapid, relatively effective, silent readers seem to be distracted and disrupted by the necessity of encoding oral output while they are decoding meaning. Ironically, then "poor" oral reading performance *may* reflect a high degree of reading competence rather than a lack of such competence.

---

[7] Kenneth S. Goodman and Carolyn L. Burke, *Study of Children's Behavior While Reading Orally,* Final Report, Project S 425, USOE, March 1968.

Relevance

The language user, though he may be a beginner as far as literacy is concerned, brings to the task of learning to read the sum total of his life's experiences and the language competence he has already acquired. He has learned language well no matter what rung on the socioeconomic ladder his dialect occupies. To make it possible for each learner to fully capitalize on these resources the reading curriculum must be relevant to him. It must make it possible for him to build on his strengths, not put him at a disadvantage by focusing on his weaknesses.

All learners have had experiences. A learner is only disadvantaged if the school rejects his experiences as unsuitable to build learnings on while accepting those of other children. Similarly language difference is not a disadvantage unless the school rejects certain dialects and insists that a child must speak and read in a dialect in which he is not competent.

Remedial reading classes and clinics invariably have more boys than girls, more blacks than whites, more minority group youngsters than is proportional in the population these programs serve. This is not so much an indication of real weakness in these groups as it is of the failure of school reading programs to adequately reach them.

Too much time has been spent trying to find weaknesses and deficiencies in children which might explain their lack of success in learning to read. A flexible, relevant reading curriculum would capitalize on the strengths of children of both sexes and of all shapes, sizes, colors, ethnic and cultural backgrounds, dispositions, energy levels, and physical attributes. Every objective in reading must be relevant to the pupils we are teaching.

Comprehension: The Prime Objective in Reading

Essentially, the only objective in reading is comprehension. All else is either a skill to be used in achieving comprehension (for example, selecting key graphic cues), a subcategory of comprehension (for example, critical reading) or a use to be made of comprehension (e.g., appreciation of literature).

Comprehension depends on the successful processing of three kinds of information: grapho-phonic, syntactic, and semantic. A series of abilities is necessary to make this process successful. How these abilities operate within this process is illustrated in the tentative Model of Reading (Figure 5).[8]

Reading instruction has as its subsidiary objectives development of these skills and strategies:

Scanning: The ability to move from left to right and down a page line by line.

Fixing: The ability to focus the eye on the line of print.

Selecting: The ability to select from graphic input those key cues which will be most productive in the information processing. For example, initial consonants are the most useful letters in words.

Predicting: The ability to predict input on the basis of grammar and growing sense of meaning from prior decoding. (Prediction and selection operate together since each is dependent on the other.)

Forming: The ability to form perceptual images on the basis of selection and prediction. The reader must combine what he sees with what he expects to see to form a perceptual image.

Searching: The ability to search memory for phonological cues and related syntactic and semantic information associated with perceptual images. The reader brings to bear his language knowledge and his experiential and conceptual background as he reads.

Tentative Choosing: The ability to make tentative choices (guesses) on the basis of minimal cues and related syntactic and semantic input. It is crucial that the reader use the least amount of information possible to make the best guess possible. To do so, he will need well developed strategies that become almost automatic.

---

[8] The author is indebted to William Gephart for the original flow chart for this model and to William Page for the current version.

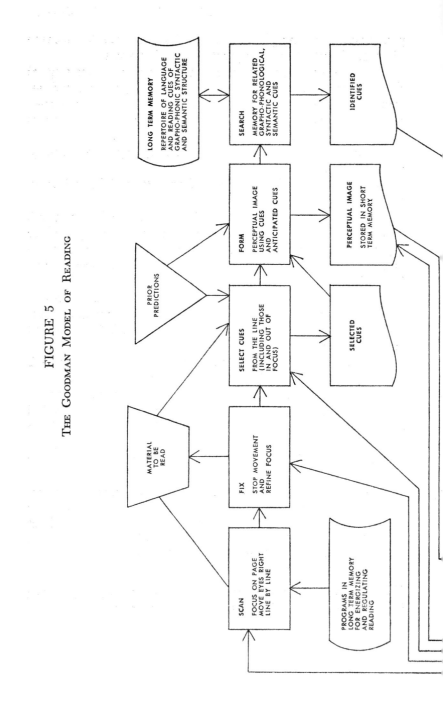

FIGURE 5

THE GOODMAN MODEL OF READING

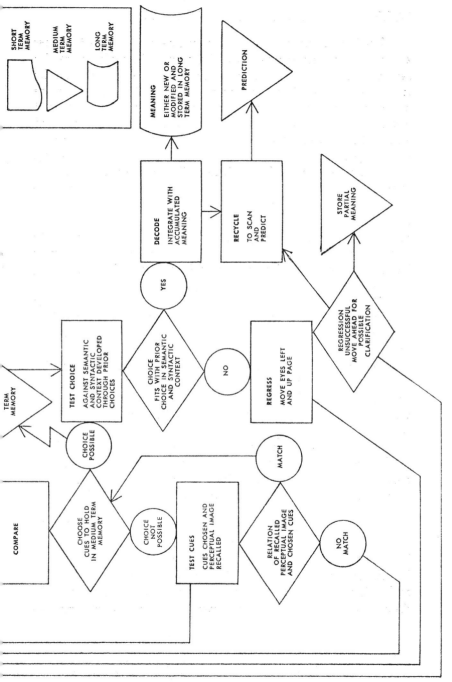

Testing—Semantic and Syntactic: The ability to test choices against the screens of meaning and grammar. Literally the reader says to himself: "Does that make sense?" "Does that sound like language to me?" This involves the crucial ability to recognize his own errors when they are significant. Readers who do not use these two screens will tend to have low comprehension and will make little effective progress in reading, though they may become good word callers (recoders in the sense defined above).

Testing—Grapho-phonic: The ability to test the tentative choice, if it has failed the prior test, against the recalled perceptual image and to gather more graphic information if needed. Note that it is only when the choice has been rejected on semantic or syntactic grounds that there is any need to resort to further grapho-phonic information. A miscalled word is most likely to be recognized as a mistake if it doesn't fit the meaning and grammar screens.

Regressing: The ability to scan right to left and up the page line by line if a choice is found unacceptable on prior tests. This involves the reader's recognizing that an anomaly or inconsistency exists in his processing to date and attempting to locate the source or point of error and then reprocessing. This is the device by which the reader corrects the errors he has recognized. A great deal of learning takes place through correction. The reader teaches himself new strategies and new insights as well as new words.

Decoding: When a successful, acceptable choice has been made, the reader integrates the information gained with the meaning which has been forming. This may involve assimilation of new meaning or accommodation of meaning previously decoded, or both.

Each of these abilities involves a set of strategies and techniques. Though phonic generalizations and sight words are learned and used in the reading process, it is the acquisition of key strategies which makes this knowledge develop and which makes it useful to the reader. In early reading instruction children will form associations between oral and written language (phonics generalizations). But only in the selection strategies, the perceptual image forming techniques, the grapho-phonic testing, and the semantic and syntactic contexts does this knowledge take on its true importance.

Some of the techniques we have tended to label word attack skills are useful. But, if we raise our sights from words to the whole reading process, these techniques will change their relative importance. Consider this short sequence:

> The boys stumbled into the house after their long hike. Mother said, "You must really be *fatigued*. Sit here and rest while I get lunch ready."

> When she returned with the food, Mother discovered they were so fatigued that they had fallen asleep.

Now, if we assume that *fatigued* is an unknown word to be "attacked," we will tend to employ phonics, structural analysis and other techniques that can work within the context of the word to achieve its recognition. This will be a problem, if, as is likely, the reader has not heard the word and therefore cannot match it with an equivalent.

If on the other hand, we are concerned about the same problem as it actually is encountered in the reading process, we will see that the meaning of the passage can come through rather clearly without the identification of this word. In fact, it is quite likely that in this short sequence the reader had become aware that the word must mean something like "tired." Should he assume another definition, *hungry* for example, subsequent reading might cause a correction. All of the syntactic and semantic information which the reader has going for him makes him relatively independent of the grapho-phonic information.

Developing Sophistication in Reading

Adequate functioning of the reading process depends on development in a number of areas, both mechanical and intellectual. A deficiency in any one of these can affect the quality of the child's reading and lessen its meaning for him.

Techniques and Strategies

If a reader does not develop independence in the use of the strategies and techniques required for adequate functioning of the reading process then special attention may be required. Cycles of skill instruction could be planned which would move the learner from language to a focus on the technique or knowledge which he needs and then back to language so that he can test the technique as he attempts to read.

To pick a simple example, suppose that a child is not aware that initial consonants are the most useful graphic cues. Instruction might help him by selecting from reading material words which start in various ways. Then the reader would return to the reading material to utilize the technique of selecting initial consonant cues.

If on the other hand children become overdependent on specific techniques, then again they can be guided within the full scope of reading materials to put the techniques in proper perspective in relationship to other techniques and available information. Suppose a child had become too reliant on initial consonants and was using neither meaning and syntax nor other graphic cues well. He could be helped to move away from his overdependence while the weak strategies were being developed at the same time.

Sequencing of skill instruction in reading has often been strongly advocated by publishers and curriculum workers. But the reading process requires that a multitude of skills be used simultaneously. As we have indicated, many of these skills are already employed by the learner in listening. *Any sequence will necessarily be arbitrary.*

Flexibility

In discussing adaptation, we indicated the need for developing general reading strategies and special reading strategies for literature, science, social studies and other language uses. The key to this development is experience of the learner with a wide variety of materials, and guidance from the teacher as it is needed to help develop specific strategies to handle the requirements of these special reading materials. This is only one kind of flexibility needed. A second kind of flexibility has to do with reading purpose. The reader needs to gain flexibility in the way his reading process functions in relation to the outcome he desires.

If he desires a high degree of comprehension with great detail then he will be more demanding of himself and more painstaking. If at the opposite extreme he is only concerned with getting a quick notion of the general drift of what he is reading, he will use test processes more freely, sample more widely, and not bother to worry about errors as he reads. If speed reading courses have any validity it must be in their ability to get readers to break out of a single inflexible reading style and into a more variable one.

A Sense of the Significance of Reading

A child who was a beginning reader was once asked why she thought it was important to know how to read. "You might park some place," she said, "and there might be a No Parking sign there. And a man might come out and say, 'Can't you read?' "

The story illustrates a small child's view of the great importance of being able to read in a literate society. An individual in a literate society has many, many encounters every day that require the comprehension of written language. Success with adult illiterates in building literacy has been achieved by building the instructional program around their most pressing needs: signs, applications, labels, directions, and other mundane things which readers take for granted.

A lesser, but still important motivation for the acquisition of reading comes from the pleasure and satisfaction it provides. This is not to say that simply by telling children how much fun reading is they can be motivated to learn. Rather, they can be led to discover this for themselves. The enjoyment of a good story will whet the appetite for more. The satisfaction of getting the information needed from a reference work will stimulate the reader to make greater use of reading as a source of information.

In aiding children to see the significance of reading, we should avoid the temptation of preselecting all the material for them. Children, like adults, have varied tastes and interests. What most children like or profit from may be totally uninteresting to one child. If a child is to find himself in reading, a wide range of topics, formats, and even quality must be represented in the material available to him.

In the multimedia world in which today's children become literate, reading need not be isolated from or exalted above other media. Television, movies, radio can and do actually stimulate reading. Today's readers have seen and heard events that their parents and grandparents encountered only through their newspapers. They bring a much broader background and range of interests to reading than any earlier generations. Above all, motivation for reading requires that schools make themselves relevant to today's children.

Critical Sense

To read critically is to read skeptically. The reader asks himself not only, "Do I understand what this means?" but "Do I buy it?" Implicit in critical reading is a set of values and criteria which is constantly brought into play throughout the process.

Three things are requisite to developing critical reading competence. First, the reader must develop a set of appropriate criteria to judge what he is reading, or at least he must have general criteria which will help him deal with matters such as plausibility, credibility, ulterior motives of the writer or publisher, and so forth. Second, he must see critical reading as necessary and possible for himself. Third, he must be aware of the devices which writers use to appeal emotionally and subtly to him as a means of influencing him.

Much of the reading required of children in school deters rather than promotes critical reading. If there is always one right answer to a question, if the teacher settles an argument by pointing out that the book has given the information on page 38 (implying that books are never wrong), if children are led to believe that they are not competent to judge the merits of their social studies or science books, then the teacher cannot turn around and ask children to read an essay in their reading text critically. One either reads critically or one does not. *The strategies required to read critically must be developed for all reading tasks and not just for special ones designed for instruction.*

Some of the most effective users of language in our country are paid high salaries by Madison Avenue agencies to convince the public that they cannot possibly exist without their clients' products. The same *tactics* have been used with remarkable success to sell political candidates. Only a truly critical reader or listener can hope to ferret out fact from propaganda.

Conclusion

Everyone agrees that reading is a critical area in education. Everyone agrees that methods must be found and curricula developed to teach all children to read effectively. Energy and money are expended for materials, clinics, special teachers by school systems and by parents. That private clinics flourish and that schools are increasing their efforts are mute evidence that the problems of reading instruction have not been solved.

The state of reading instruction today is that of an art. Skilled teachers and specialists have the know-how to help *most*, but not all, of their pupils.

There is no simple breakthrough in reading just around the corner which will change instruction to a foolproof science. As more is understood about reading and learning to read, it becomes ever clearer how complex these processes are. No simple antitoxin can be injected in nonreaders to make them readers. But progress will come as misconceptions disappear in favor of sound understanding. Materials and curricula based on scientific insights will replace those built on tradition, trial-and-error and expediency. And a reading curriculum will evolve tied to an effective theory of reading instruction.

The basis for such progress now exists. If parents, teachers and administrators can resist simplistic panaceas and keep up sustained efforts to achieve more effective reading instruction then the next decade can be the one in which the major problems are solved.

School Programs: The Necessary Conditions

Focusing on the secondary school: appropriate climates for reading, development of curriculum, recent trends, evaluation of organizational structure, teacher selection and preparation, and materials

Part 2
By Olive S. Niles

SCHOOL PROGRAMS:
The Necessary Conditions

The better our understanding of the processes of reading and of learning to read, as decribed in the preceding pages, the more marvelous it seems that most children become, in varying degrees, masters of the act of reading. It may well be the most difficult task human beings ever face, yet we expect the five- or six-year-old to understand the first and most fundamental components of the act.

So complex a task will probably never be easy for a child to accomplish, but educators, recognizing the crucial importance of skill in reading as a basic tool in all aspects and at all levels of education, have expended their energy in trying to find ways to make it relatively easier.

Six general approaches to the problem have been pursued. The first of these has been explored in depth in Part 1 of this monograph; the remaining five will be discussed in the following pages:

1. better understanding of the nature of the reading process itself;
2. attention to the climate (classroom, school, community) in which a reading program can operate to the best advantage;

3. construction and revision of curriculum;
4. study of organizational structures for teaching reading within a single classroom or within a school or school system;
5. better selection and preparation of teachers; and
6. improvements in instructional materials and procedures for using them.

Climate

The climate in which a reading program is developed has as much effect upon its success as the weather has on the growth of a plant. It has been said that the 1960s have brought into prominence the importance of the affective factors in education. How pupils and teachers feel—a result of the climate in which they work—may be as important as what they know. Recent developments, especially studies of culturally deprived children, have also emphasized the importance of another aspect of the educational environment: vivid sensory stimulation of all kinds, not just the visual.

Atmosphere, favorable or unfavorable, exists in the individual classroom, in the school as a whole, in the community. Of course, it affects every part of the school program, but perhaps the area of reading more than anything else. If a pupil's spelling is poor or if he can't throw a ball very well, neither parent nor pupil is likely to be very much concerned about the matter. Mothers have been heard to say with a shrug and a smile, "Oh, well, his father never could spell either!" But they never seem to make this kind of remark about learning to read. It means too much to them.

Affective Climate

What are the characteristics which make up an affective climate in which teachers are happy and pupils grow strong in reading?

The most essential element is a feeling of security and success. Even the strongest individual will, after awhile, be defeated by failure, whether he is a pupil of six, or one of eighteen, a beginning teacher or a veteran. The ego suffers from constant failure, and, when it does, the struggle to learn or to teach no longer seems worthwhile. The individual may just go limp and drift along with the least possible effort or he may, if he has a stronger personality, exhibit an aggressively negative reaction to a situation which he finds intolerable. All successful teachers have ways of building ego-strength in their pupils. All successful supervisors and administrators can do the same in working with their teachers. They seek strengths and build more strength on existing strength.

Another very important element in a good climate for a reading program is a carefully nourished conviction that learning to read is very important and worthwhile. Because students of any age have a very limited view of future benefits to be derived from such a program, it is of no use to tell them, "You won't get into college if you can't read well" or "reading is very important if you want to have a good job someday." They must see that reading is important right now. Teachers must make very sure pupils know why they are learning how to skim, or to read for main ideas, or to divide words into syllables. Of what use are these skills? Pupils must see exactly how some lesson they have to do is made easier because they have these skills. Too often only teachers see this; it should be no secret to the pupils.

Furthermore, of course, the pupils should have plenty of enjoyment in reading. They must listen to stories well read—in grade twelve as well as grade one—they must have experiences in dramatization, they must participate joyfully in choral reading, they must spend relaxed time just browsing and reading in a friendly, cheerful library setting. Some schools are setting aside periods of time each week for pupils to do any kind of independent reading they may wish to do. As the pleasure mounts so does the skill, or at least it seems to do so. Perhaps the students are simply more willing to *use* skills they had all the time.

The climate of secondary schools has often been unfavorable to a reading program for a number of reasons. One is the attitude of some content teachers, which they make very clear to their students, that reading should be taught in the elementary school and that something is wrong either with the student himself or with his elementary school experience if he does not read as well as his fellows. Secondary teachers who have this attitude fail to realize or to accept the fact that even the most capable children in elementary school are not mature enough to grasp the more advanced levels of many essential skills. Furthermore, few of the skills have been learned, by the end of grade six, so well that no further teaching or practice is necessary.

Of course, all content teachers use reading in their classes, but they too often feel no obligation to teach it or even to support the efforts of reading teachers who are trying to teach it. This negative attitude does much to discourage not only the reading teachers but also those students who may be receiving reading instruction. All secondary teachers need to realize that knowledge of specific content is of far less importance to the student than strong, positive attitudes toward learning and toward mastery of the skills that will make it possible for him to go on learning as long as he lives. Youngsters in secondary schools today will spend a good portion of their lives in the twenty-first century. By that time most of the facts they are learning in school will be obsolete or incomplete; if they have not learned how to learn, they will be handicapped indeed.

Not that reading is the only way to learn: it is only one of the best ways. Therefore, one of the major responsibilities of every secondary content teacher is to teach students in all his classes efficient ways to read and study in his particular field. These ways may differ considerably from efficient ways to study in some other field. This fact is a major reason why no one group of teachers should be responsible for teaching developmental reading in the secondary school. It has been customary in many schools to associate the teaching of reading exclusively or mainly with the English department. Once this association is made, other content teachers tend to assume that they have no responsibility in the matter. This assumption is very difficult to remove once it is established. In building a secondary reading program, every effort should be made to involve all departments from the start.

Climate favorable to reading is always a matter of how people feel about reading. It grows from positive, energizing attitudes of teachers who build the same attitudes in their pupils. It results in emotional security and strong stimulation which make the student reach and stretch because he is eager to grow. He recognizes this favorable climate in the kind of questioning the teacher uses. Really important questions are never fully answered; they always raise more questions and stimulate students to start in pursuit of more answers. In a classroom which has the right atmosphere, students do not have to put up with routine practice work which furnishes no zest, no inspiration to perform at a high level.

Physical Climate

Of less importance than the affective climate is the physical setting for a good reading program, but the surroundings can also be highly stimulating. A visitor aware of what to look for can tell in a few minutes the degree to which a classroom or an entire school is geared to reading. Everywhere there are signs that pupils are reading and doing things with their reading.

First of all, the library/media center is comfortable, spacious, well-stocked, and, above all, busy. The librarian may have had to put temporary cards into the latest shipment of books because the pupils *have* to have them before she has found time to process them. Pupils are constantly in and out of the library, singly, in small study groups, as whole classes, before school, after school, all day. In the corridors the student-made bulletin boards are direct evidence of reading going on: newspaper clippings on the latest space happenings, experience charts about a trip to Forest Park, a have-you-read-this display to which individual pupils attach notes about books that are just too good *not* to read. In the classrooms, centers of interest and display areas raise questions and suggest explorations which lead pupils to reading. A classroom library managed and arranged by the pupils themselves and frequently changed brings them even closer to books than the central library and makes reading more "special." Teachers are readers themselves and share their own enthusiasms for reading with the pupils, encouraging them sometimes to read the very same books and share their feelings in an adult-to-adult fashion very stimulating to pupils' egos. Teachers' reading is often visible to pupils in the form, for example, of a book or magazine picked up in an odd moment or a book tucked under the arm when the teacher leaves for the day. Though the era when the teacher was always a model to be emulated seems to be long gone, it still makes good sense to let pupils see him do what he says *they* should do.

A reading climate of this sort is too infrequent in elementary schools; it is rare in secondary schools. It is true, of course, that for young adults the physical environment must differ from that found in elementary schools. Secondary students are too self-conscious to respond to the personal appeal of having their work displayed or their recommendations posted for all to see. But the bare four walls of the all-too-typical secondary classroom are surely no inducement to read. Secondary school teachers are finding that classroom collections of paperbacks are an effective lure into worthwhile books. Subject matter in such collections should not be limited to English, though it often is. Secondary libraries are adding special browsing areas with comfortable furniture and inviting displays which suggest that libraries are for pleasure as well as plenty of hard work. In these browsing areas are books, of course, but also the really popular magazines: *Seventeen, Look, Hot Rod, Ebony,* and many more.

Secondary students who need remedial help are particularly sensitive to their situation. By this time, if their problems are serious, they are frustrated, often hostile, and, unless they have very active support, ready to give up the struggle. They see themselves as having to be on the defensive in order to maintain integrity in their own eyes. The person, however, who sees himself as stupid has learned this concept; and *learned* behavior can be adjusted and modified. For this reason the atmosphere of the remedial area is vital. Some schools are making this area especially attractive, perhaps the most comfortable room or rooms in the whole school, with good facilities for individual study and at least a few of the teaching machines (which may serve their most useful purpose in such a setting). Most important is the teacher. Preferably he is a vigorous, athletic type of man. Most of his students will be boys who need to associate reading with a strong male image. His understanding and patience must know no bounds and his skill as a reading teacher must be equally outstanding. In such an environment there is hope even for the most discouraged students.

Climate of the Community

Climate within the school is crucial, but it cannot be maintained without a corresponding climate in the community. Former U.S. Commissioner of Education James E. Allen proposed that underachievement in reading be wiped out in this country during the 1970s. This proposal is not new; probably every school system in the country has stated such a goal— though usually without attaching a date! What chance is there that it could be achieved? A very good chance if the attitude is right in the community—local, state, national. It is ridiculous to believe that this country can put men on the moon and not wipe out reading deficiencies if enough people decide it is the thing to do and will support it. It hasn't been done in the past for lack of determination and dedication. At the very least, success will require vast sums of money and the commitment of a tremendous amount of professional energy. The most important developments it will involve are these:

- a program to wipe out completely the handicap under which bright but socially and emotionally deprived children start school. (Head Start is only a beginning);
- substantial reduction in class size, especially in the primary grades, and/or substantial increase in the number

of personnel, some of them paraprofessionals, who will work in teams with larger groups of children;
- major changes in the preservice education of teachers, one of these changes being the requirement that *all* prospective teachers, including secondary teachers in all content areas, take at least one course in methods of teaching reading;
- a program of inservice training for thousands of practicing teachers, for which they will have to be compensated;
- the development of a large corps of specialists in reading whose business will be training teachers, both preservice and inservice; and
- an intensive public relations program to convince boards of education and taxpayers that they can and should support such a task.

Curriculum: Current Trends

The word *curriculum* may encompass everything that happens to a student, in school and out, by means of which he has the opportunity to learn. However, in this monograph it will be used to mean the plan which has been conceived to give structure and order to an educational program. A viable plan has a good deal to do with the success of the reading program.

Too often the curriculum in reading is the basal reading series in use in the community or, in a secondary school, a similar set of books. Many of these books are well thought out and carefully written, but they do not serve as a good curriculum. They are merely the tools with which it can be implemented. A good curriculum is planned directly for a given group of students whose backgrounds and future goals are known to the planners or can be fairly accurately predicted. It takes into consideration the resources of the community, the strengths of the professional staff, and the amount of paraprofessional help that can be made available.

Curriculum documents can be brief, consisting mainly of a statement of goals, or they can be very detailed including many suggestions for teaching procedures and materials. Length is not a criterion of quality. Curriculum writers must consider what kind of plan is needed and will be used. For example, in a community which has an outstanding staff of consultants in reading, a lengthy spelling out of procedures and materials is a waste of time; the main reason consultants exist is to supply this kind of know-how at the moment it is needed. Conversely, teachers in a small school system with little or no consultant help and, perhaps, far removed from colleges or universities where teachers can take courses to help them keep up to date might be better off with a more detailed document, provided administrative attitudes encouraged them to use it.

Three trends in curriculum development in reading can be clearly identified.

The first of these is a trend toward the statement of goals in terms of behavioral objectives on an ungraded continuum. There is far from general agreement that a curriculum should be so constructed, but the procedure seems to be most defensible in an area like reading in which fairly easily definable and measurable skills play so prominent a role. Persons who argue for this kind of statement contend that a teacher who does not know as exactly as possible what the end product of his effort should look like will never know whether he has achieved his goal. As an illustration, a few statements which might appear somewhere on a continuum concerned with the ability to understand and use the concept of main ideas and related details follow.

Given lists which contain one main topic and both related and unrelated details, the student will be able to select the main topic and the related details, discarding the unrelated.

Given paragraphs concerning concepts which are familiar to him, the student will be able to select from a list of four summary sentences following each paragraph the central idea of the paragraph and to identify each of the three distractors as too broad, too narrow, or off the subject.

The student will be able to identify topic sentences in paragraphs which concern concepts familiar to him, wherever the topic sentence may be located in the paragraph, and will also be able to identify paragraphs which contain no stated topic sentences.

The student will be able to construct in standard form a two-level outline of three related paragraphs which deal with concepts familiar to him.

In a curriculum of this type, goals in each of the areas of skills-development (word analysis, oral reading skills, etc.) are arranged in approximate order of their difficulty of attainment. There is very little research in connection with most of the skills to support such an ordering of the levels of difficulty; it has to be based on common sense, and committees working on such statements of behavioral objectives will not always agree. However, such a list serves a practical purpose. By the end of grade twelve, it would be hoped that behavior of the majority of students would approximate the final goal in the sequence, but, because the continuum is ungraded, adjustments to individual differences can be made all along the way and the pitfalls of minimum grade standards can be avoided. Such statements of behavioral goals are strengthened if they are accompanied by suggested means of evaluation which may be used to determine whether students have actually achieved each goal. Evaluative criteria must be planned to test the pupil's use of the skill, not merely his ability to parrot what he has learned.

A second trend in curriculum development is toward a broad involvement of many persons in the process. At long last, the consumers are really being asked to help: the students themselves and those most concerned with results, among them parents and adults in the community into whose employ these young people will go. Within the school, teachers, administrators, reading consultants, audiovisual specialists, counselors, librarians—all are being asked to help determine what a reading curriculum for a given school or school system should look like. Involving many people is one way to make everyone feel somewhat responsible for what develops, and in an all-pervasive area like reading this involvement is crucial. The process may be slow, and the reading consultant, one of whose major responsibilities is to see that curriculum *does* evolve, often wishes he could sit down in his office, close the door, and write it himself, but this is the best way to insure that the document will gather dust.

Curriculum in reading is, in the third place, gradually becoming a unified plan from the prereading stage through grade 12 or grade 14. (Note the term "prereading," which is no longer synonymous with a kindergarten or first-grade readiness program. Prereading preparation is beginning as early as age four and may, if some theorists prevail, be moved into still earlier stages of the child's development.) In such unified curriculum planning, some of the serious breaks in continuity, such as that between sixth grade and junior high school, are healed. Ungradedness, which is becoming fairly common in elementary schools and is even being cautiously implemented in a few secondary schools, lends support to this concept of an unbroken continuum, as does the trend toward individualized instruction, which will be discussed later.

Organizational Structure

If we take as the all-inclusive goal of all reading instruction that every pupil be capable of performing at his potential level and motivated to do so, it is probable that we could come very close to this goal—if the teacher could instruct every student individually. However, even under these ideal conditions, a few might not respond because of hidden causes for failure which have not yet been identified.

However, since the cost factor makes individual tutoring prohibitive, teachers must work within some kind of groupings. The problem becomes one of determining what kinds of organization are most effective under given conditions, and since "given conditions" vary so widely it is unlikely that any general organizational pattern will or could emerge as optimum. The two questions which should be asked about all organizational structure, however, are clear.

What structure will provide the greatest degree of attention to individual differences without sacrificing the values of group interaction in reading instruction?

What structure will provide the best teaching of reading *per se* without sacrificing the transfer of skills and attitudes from reading instruction to the multiple uses of reading in the various disciplines and in life itself?

Obviously, the phrase "without sacrificing" implies carefully considered compromises in, or combinations of, instructional organization. For example, individualized instruction of any type, if carried to an extreme, would not only make learning to read a very lonely process but probably also would result in superficial learning. It is in the group interchange of ideas and reactions about what is about to be read or what has been read that pupils develop depth of insight. A typical comment which reveals this added insight is "I would never have thought of that!" Similarly, the Joplin plan, which involves the interclass grouping of children homogeneously according to reading level and sometimes across grade lines, may have its advantages in terms of the learning of the skills, since it is likely to provide increased and intensified teaching of these skills. At the same time, it may decrease the amount of transfer of the skills, transfer for which the self-contained classroom provides an ideal setting.

Too often a new organizational pattern has been inaugurated because teachers or administrators have seen in it some single strength and have not gone beyond this observation to analyze possible adverse effects. For example, departmentalization in the elementary school may make excellent use of teacher time and competency but at the same time sacrifice attention to individual differences because a teacher simply cannot understand a hundred children in the same depth he can understand twenty-five.

Trends in Organizational Structure

Organizational structure for the teaching of reading is presently very fluid in the schools, so much so that it is difficult even to identify definite trends, much less evaluate them. Recent events, including racial integration, have tended to halt or reverse a trend toward tracking or homogeneous grouping which had become very common, particularly in secondary schools. Individualization of instruction, on the other hand, is receiving much attention. Electronic devices now on the market are encouraging this individualization, though at such a high price that devices such as the talking typewriter and computerized instruction are actually in use with only a few children. Instruction with somewhat more conventional materials such as those prepared for Individually Prescribed Instruction [1] and PLAN,[2] both of which are now available commercially, is less costly but is still considered experimental. Instruction of the type popularized by Veatch [3] is widely practiced, particularly as a supplement to basal programs. Individualized reading of the Veatch type stresses self-selection. A very different kind of individualization is featured in programed instruction (for example, the Sullivan materials).[4] In this type the pupil has very little freedom of selection; individualization resides in the rate at which he is able to absorb the material, each student progressing through it at his individual speed. Thus, most programed material is prescriptive of everything but the time element.

In secondary schools modular scheduling, elective courses, and independent study programs are appearing. They are clearly the result of a conviction that offerings in any area, including reading, which are designed for a whole school or even a large segment within a school (such, for example, as two periods per week of instruction in reading for every student in grades seven and eight) fall far short of providing for individuals. When one

---

[1] *Individually Prescribed Instruction,* a special report by *Education U.S.A.,* 1201 16th Street, N.W., Washington, D.C., 1968.

[2] William Shanner, *PLAN, a System of Individualized Instruction,* published by Westinghouse Learning Corporation, 100 Park Ave., New York, New York.

[3] Jeannette Veatch, *Individualizing Your Reading Program* (New York: G. P. Putnam's Sons, 1959).

[4] Programed materials by M. W. Sullivan have been published by the McGraw-Hill Book Company and by Behavioral Research Laboratories.

looks at all of these developments, one sees behind them as the major impetus a surge of reaction against conventional group instruction.

The second major trend in organizational structure which seems to be observable, though less clearly so, perhaps, in reading instruction than in some other areas, might be described as an effort to capitalize on teachers' strengths—strengths in a broader sense than mere subject matter competence. Under the loose heading of team teaching, many imaginative ways to use teacher competence are being investigated, some of them resulting in very complex organizational structures. A simple example is the team teaching arrangement in elementary schools which pairs just two teachers: the classroom teacher and the corrective reading teacher. Since the beginning of remedial reading instruction, small groups of pupils or individuals have been taken out of classrooms and tutored in a special program parallel to and usually only remotely related to the program within the classroom. If the two teachers involved consulted at all with each other, consultation was usually unsystematic and infrequent.

Currently some school systems are teaming these two teachers, encouraging the corrective teacher to do her work in the classroom itself for a period of time each day while the classroom teacher is working with other children in the same room. Thus constant daily contact between the two teachers is maintained and the corrective teacher is strongly encouraged to conduct a program which directly reinforces the work of the classroom. One effect of this teaming is to make a whole school more reading conscious. Teachers discuss reading; they are more interested in new materials for teaching reading and more conscious of individual needs of children. In this relationship, as in all aspects of team teaching, new building construction which provides open space and few permanent walls is important but not essential. If teachers are convinced of its importance, team teaching can be implemented in almost any kind of building.

In the secondary school, team teaching in reading is just beginning to be developed. This is much more difficult to implement because of the generations of experience with tightly compartmentalized subject matter units. Reading teachers have a very hard time relating themselves to the traditional kind of department organization because their goals are basically different from those of content teachers. They offer a program which should support all departments and not, under any circumstances, exist as a separate entity. Yet separation of effort exists in all but a few secondary school reading programs. The reading "department" is comparatively new in secondary schools, and it has, in most instances, been brought in to coexist with other departments in the school as if it had similar goals and could operate in similar ways. It cannot because it is cross-disciplinary and must work with all departments. Thus, the slowly emerging trend toward team teaching (the term is used very loosely here) in secondary schools presents an opportunity for reading teachers to assume a role which is honest and helpful.

Imagine, if you will, a situation in which a group of four teachers of the major disciplines (English, social studies, science, mathematics) become responsible for one hundred students. To this team is added a full-time reading teacher if the students need a great deal of help. If the students need less help, the reading teacher may share his time, perhaps on a weekly basis, with another team of four teachers. The reading teacher works with the team in these ways:

- He participates in many, if not all, of their planning sessions, thus being very clearly aware of what the students are being asked to read and for what purposes.
- He goes into classrooms for all or parts of periods, as determined in the planning sessions, and teaches, using the regular materials of the classroom but stressing *how* to read and study them as well as their content.
- He diagnoses needs of individual students and may, on occasion, take them out of regular classes for special instruction or suggest to the classroom teachers ways to help a student compensate for his weaknesses.
- He examines the teaching materials to determine their suitability to the reading levels of the pupils and suggests other or supplementary materials as needed.

Under this type of organizational structure the reading teacher becomes an integral part of the on-going process of education and not a disassociated adjunct. Furthermore, and more important, students understand why they are asked to work on certain skills because, when they work with what they consider "real" content lessons, they can see the immediate and fruitful effect of their efforts.

Evaluating Organizational Structure

These two trends in organizing reading programs are important: individualizing of instruction with its many ramifications and better uses of reading teacher time and competence. Most of the innovative practices now current are related in some fashion to one or the other of them.

All changes in organizational structure of the reading program are, of course, intimately related to all other aspects of the school program and must be evaluated not only in terms of what they contribute to the teaching of reading *per se* but also in terms of what they do to the total school program. It may be that a reading program should embrace more than one pattern of organization. Some pupils seem to do better in a tight, formal structure; for others, the reverse is true. Teachers, also, are not alike in this respect. Organization could, and perhaps should, become very complex even within a single school.

Evaluative criteria may well include the following:

the degree to which a particular organizational structure improves the chances that individual students will get the kind of instruction they need;

the degree to which it will insure that students have the opportunity to use the skills they are learning;

the degree to which it will make the best use of teacher competencies;

the effect it has on pupil motivation to learn to read better; and

the per-pupil cost to implement.

Selection and Preparation of Teachers

Since the publication of the first-grade studies sponsored in 1965 and 1966 by the U.S. Office of Education,[5] it has been common in reading circles to say that "the teacher is the thing." These studies clearly indicated that differences in the performance of children, at least in grade one, depend more on the teacher than on the type of reading program or materials involved—and practically every kind of first-grade reading program was tested somewhere in the various studies.

The best of plans and materials in inept hands can be wasted. It is, therefore, of the greatest importance that the recruitment of prospective teachers as well as both their preservice and their inservice training be of the best possible type.

Recruitment of Teachers

Two factors affect the recruitment of teachers directly: salary prospects and working conditions. Although teachers' salaries have improved a great deal in the last few years, they still do not attract the most able students in the best colleges and universities. Salaries must be comparable to those in industry and the other professions before this conditions will be corrected. Also, salary schedules will have to be more flexible in order to reward more fully those who continue to improve their teaching skills through further graduate study and experience. The single salary schedule tends to promote mediocrity.

Conditions for teaching will also have to be improved. Teachers must have all the materials they need, pleasant, uncrowded space in which to work, supportive relationships with supervisors and administrators, and freedom from the fears which are now current especially in many urban areas. Given these conditions, which do not presently exist in the majority of school

---

[5] Russell G. Stauffer, ed., *The First Grade Reading Studies: Findings of Individual Investigations* (Newark, Delaware: International Reading Association, 1967).

systems, all teachers can be expected to undertake preservice and inservice preparation for their work with the degree of personal sacrifice and hard work which are presently characteristic only of the best teachers.

Preservice Preparation of Reading Teachers

Successful instruction requires much more background than the so-called "methods in reading" course. The person who teaches reading at any grade level (including classroom teachers in self-contained classrooms in elementary schools and content teachers in secondary schools) should possess basic understandings at least in the following fields: psychology of personality and of learning, sociology, linguistics and psycholinguistics, measurement, and literature. Teachers who are to assume specialized roles in the reading program, particularly those who will deal with atypical pupils, need to go well beyond basic understandings. It has not yet been fully realized that disciplines other than education must be involved in the preparation of specialists in the teaching of reading. The disciplines of clinical psychology and medicine are most obvious.

Understanding of the total learning process, the effect of emotionality upon the pupil's ability to learn, and the modern theory of intelligence are all necessary to understanding the process of teaching reading at any level. Recently, the emphasis upon preschool learning and upon the development of perceptual and motor abilities not formerly closely associated with learning to read has made knowledge of up-to-date psychological theory of increasing importance.

It has always been apparent that one of the reasons why some pupils learn to read less easily than others has to do with negative forces in their social environment. Increased attention to compensatory activities to counteract the effects of these forces has made it necessary for the teacher of reading to understand the effect upon language development of different kinds of handicapping home environments: the economically deprived home, the bilingual home, etc.

Part 1 of this monograph has presented very convincingly the rationale for a study of various aspects of linguistics as a background for teaching reading. The teacher cannot expect to understand many of the new materials being published or the procedures for teaching them without at least one basic course in linguistic theory.

Almost daily measurement is necessary in a skill-building subject such as reading. Interpretation of standardized test results is impossible without knowledge of how such tests are made and what legitimate purposes they can serve. Also, the process of creating and using informal tests is of great importance to a skills teacher.

And, of course, reading is not just a skills subject. If we do not succeed in making students enthusiastic about books as well as able to read them, we have accomplished very little. Just as everyone is likely to walk away from the clerk in the department store who doesn't know his merchandise, so children walk mentally away from their teachers when these teachers don't know *their* merchandise: the literature they are teaching the children to read. "Literature" in this context has broad meaning ranging from the daily paper to the classics. Courses in children's literature and in literature for young adults help to make the reading teacher comfortable with books pupils will enjoy. Whatever a teacher at any grade level wants his pupils to read, he has to know himself. Otherwise, there is little hope he can be much of a salesman.

Many persons and groups have made proposals concerning preparation and accreditation of teachers of reading. Most important of these proposals seem to be those included in the two Harvard-Carnegie Reports [6] and the statements of the International Reading Association.[7] Such statements are indeed impor-

---

[6] Mary C. Austin and others, *The Torch Lighters: Tomorrow's Teachers of Reading* (Cambridge, Mass.: Harvard University Press, 1961). Mary C. Austin and others, *The First R: The Harvard Report on Reading in Elementary Schools* (New York: Macmillan Co., 1963).

[7] International Reading Association, "Roles, Responsibilities, and Qualifications of Reading Specialists," *Journal of Reading* 12, no. 1 (October 1968): 60-63.

tant, but it would appear that too little attention has been paid to them outside the reading profession itself. Kinder found in a 1968 survey that half of the states still permitted a so-called "reading specialist" to work with little or no training or experience.[8] Furthermore, Kinder's statement refers to the preparation and accreditation of specialists in reading. In actual practice, at least in elementary schools, most of the teaching of reading is done by generalists. In the secondary schools, a good reading program should be based in all the content fields. So far, little or no attention has been paid to adequate training of content teachers for this responsibility except, to a limited extent, prospective teachers of English.

Many colleges and universities are giving serious thought to this problem of preservice preparation, especially since surveys have indicated clearly that beginning teachers themselves are dissatisfied with their preparation. Among other developments, two are especially important. The first of these is the increasing effort to teach preservice courses through face-to-face experience with pupils rather than or in addition to the textbook-lecture-examination approach. Teachers probably cannot learn to "read" children in any other way, and they cannot teach reading unless they can "read" children. The specific practicum (microteaching), as compared to the generalized practice-teaching assignment, is receiving increasing emphasis. Undergraduates are being placed in classrooms to do short, carefully observed bits of teaching, such as a directed reading lesson. This teaching is sometimes recorded on film or videotape, sometimes observed through one-way glass. Later it can be discussed with a group of the prospective teacher's peers or with the supervisor alone. The undergraduate's chief difficulty and, incidentally, the reason for his boredom in the traditional methods course is that he can't visualize what the lecturer is talking about; he can't evaluate or react. Only after he has tried it himself—or, as a rather poor com-

---

[8] Robert Farrar Kinder, "State Certification of Reading Teachers and Specialists," *Journal of Reading* 12, no. 1 (October 1968): 9-12, 68-71.

promise, observed a master teacher perform, can he begin to understand what the methods course is all about.

The second significant development is the beginning of efforts to set behavioral goals in preservice training of teachers of reading. This calls for the same kind of definition and analysis which is called for in setting behavioral goals for youngsters. What kinds of activities must a teacher of reading be able to perform? Can these be precisely and comprehensively described? Can procedures be set up for objectively evaluating performance in relation to each of these goals? Is it possible that one prospective teacher could achieve a given goal in a week or less while another might have to practice many times before his performance could be approved? Must there be some lecturing to establish basic theory? If so, how much? Can the identification of behavioral goals be used to individualize preservice preparation and make it not only more effective but more palatable? These and probably other questions must be answered before this emerging trend in preservice education can be generally accepted.

Inservice Preparation

What of the thousands of teachers who have not had good preservice preparation for teaching reading and who are not likely to get it voluntarily? One possible answer is to make it mandatory that such teachers go back to college for graduate work—a drastic approach and one not likely to be well received even if money for tuition were made available.

What, also, of teachers who have had good preservice training but who have done little to keep up with the rapid changes that are occurring? No college, no matter how good its preservice program, can prepare teachers for a lifetime of teaching any more than it can prepare doctors for a lifetime of doctoring. The medical profession seems to have accepted this fact; the teaching profession as a whole has not.

Inservice training is probably the answer. It has one great advantage over the typical university course. Because it is local, it can be tailored to a particular situation. Thus its goals are clearer and often more practical.

Apart from a lack of recognition of the need for it, the growth of good inservice training has been slow for two reasons. First, it costs a good deal of money. It requires the services of expert and expensive consultant help and few communities have enough personnel to provide anything like the amount of service that is needed. There should be at least one resident consultant for every one hundred teachers, including elementary school classroom teachers and secondary content teachers. Even more expensive is the overtime pay for teachers to take advantage of workshops, lectures, demonstrations, visitations, and other activities necessary to a good inservice program.

The second reason for the slow growth of effective inservice training is the time element. Although, if enough consultants are available, a good deal can be done to help teachers in their classrooms during school hours, there must also be time when they can meet in groups in a relaxed atmosphere to learn from a consultant, to evaluate materials, to share with each other, even to read the professional literature. Many school systems are experimenting with, or at least beginning to consider, the twelve-month year with ten months of teaching, one month of inservice work of some type, and one month of vacation. In such a program as this, much better use can be made of consultant time if the month of inservice training is rotated through the year with different groups of teachers available to work with the consultant for different periods of time—not all in the month of July!

Procedures for inservice work with teachers can be as varied as the imagination of the consultant and his sensitivity to teacher need and readiness permit. There are certain broad guidelines which should be considered:

1. The more specific the emphasis, the better. Teachers react much better to short, intensive study of a particular problem they have recognized than to a broad frontal attack on everything at once. Immediate relevance is essential. Consequently, it is usually unwise to attempt

inservice work with broadly heterogeneous groups of teachers; for example, teachers K-12 all meeting in the same sessions, beginning teachers meeting with veterans, teachers of the disadvantaged meeting with teachers of the gifted.

2. The more activity on the part of the teachers involved, the better—activity with pupils, with books or other materials, with visits to see something new or different. If they are somehow on the move, they are interested.

3. The more involvement of teachers in planning the inservice work, the better. They may not know as well as the consultant what they need, but they definitely know what they can accept.

4. The more immediate the application in the classroom, the better. If such application does not result, the inservice program has been a failure, no matter how carefully it was planned.

This monograph can suggest only a few of the specific ways in which inservice work has been done successfully. One of the best of these is the team teaching, discussed above. In any situation in which a skilled reading teacher can be teamed with other teachers less skilled in this particular field, there is potential for inservice growth. Umans describes a more formal project of this type.[9] In the large New York City system, reading consultants operated in teams in the junior high schools, working with content teachers of less than five years of experience. The procedure was simple. A demonstration lesson taught by the consultant was followed by a conference with the content teacher, in which the consultant helped the content teacher to understand what had been done in the demonstration and to plan another lesson. The content teacher conducted this second lesson with the reading consultant observing. This was followed by another conference and then a repetition of the cycle, the goal being to help the content teacher to see how, with the use of his own content materials, he could teach reading-study skills and

[9] Shelley Umans, *New Trends in Reading Instruction* (New York: Bureau of Publications, Teachers College, Columbia University, 1963), pp. 14-15.

content simultaneously. In the case of the Umans program the consultants stayed in a given junior high school for six consecutive weeks and then moved to another school to start a similar program. More ideally, they would be able to stay as long as they were needed to help the content teachers assume a permanent role in the reading program.

The assignment described above is a difficult one for the reading consultant because not only does he encounter the natural resistance of the content teacher to an unfamiliar program, but also he may find himself working in a content field in which he is not secure himself. This would be particularly true at the senior high level where content materials become really complex. A possible solution to this problem would involve assigning a reading consultant only to teams of teachers who work in the subject field in which the consultant himself is fully competent.

Demonstration lessons are common procedure for inservice training. A single isolated demonstration can be almost totally useless, however, unless it is directed to a specific problem which a teacher or group of teachers has identified. On the other hand, it may be very useful to stage a series of demonstration lessons in which the consultant can show the full cycle of diagnostic teaching and in which he can work with the same group of pupils long enough to remove the artificiality of the single encounter.

Other types of inservice procedures may be listed briefly:

A workshop for principals. In large systems, it is often hard for the consultant to reach all the teachers directly. He must work indirectly through principals. But there is a more important reason to consider a workshop for principals. The reading program in any school will be only as good as the principal allows it to be, and many administrators know very little about this complex field. Few of them have taken a course dealing with recent trends and materials in the teaching of reading, and their own teaching experience in most instances has given them a very limited view of the total reading program.

Live educational TV and/or videotape. The lesson may be directed to pupils and observed by teachers who will be given instructions for following up the lesson in their own classrooms. Such a lesson can set an example of superior teaching. Indeed, the teachers may learn more than the students who participate. TV may also, of course, be beamed directly to the teachers themselves. In this case, it should be accompanied by teacher handbooks constructed to prepare teachers for viewing and to motivate them to use what they have seen.

Use of summer reading programs. Specially trained reading teachers may conduct summer classes with other teachers serving as assistants. The teacher-assistants will, in this way, learn new techniques of teaching.

Use of outside consultants. This is effective only in bringing information to a local group. Outside consultants should never be expected to solve local problems unless they can almost become "local" by living for considerable periods of time with the people and situations involved.

Short-term teacher involvement in reading clinics or remedial classes. Teachers who need to learn more about teaching reading can be released to spend a short time each day in such a setting watching the remedial teacher and participating in the teaching.

Reading curriculum workshops. No worthwhile curriculum development can take place without a review of the existing curriculum and investigation of possibilities for improvement. Both of these activities inevitably involve teachers in personal growth.

Films on teaching techniques. The films produced under Project English at Syracuse University are an example. They are accompanied by guides which help teachers to focus on concepts and techniques illustrated in the films.

The telelecture, by means of which even very small school systems can hear and talk back to national experts. The possibility also exists that dial-access tape banks will be organized at strategic points throughout the country. Teachers will be able to dial into these banks to hear lectures and discussions on a great variety of topics.

Use of innovative practices or materials. While no one would innovate for innovation's sake, it is true that innovation creates a felt need for inservice work and the opportunity should not be missed. Teachers get into ruts. They can be lifted out of them by change which makes them think and prepare, not just coast along.

Board of education support for additional college work. Particularly in small communities where consultants to do demonstrations, organize workshops, etc., are not available, this kind of support may be in the long run the most economical way for the community to help some of its teachers to grow on the job.

Bulletins. Wastebaskets are so handy that bulletins have to be very, very good indeed to make much of an impression, but they are always a possibility.

Instructional Materials

Many teachers will indicate that they could do a much better job of implementing a reading program if they had better materials. Probably they attach too much importance to materials—good teachers can and often have taught children to read well with very poor materials, even with materials far too difficult for the children. The *sine qua non* is the teacher, not the book.

However, good materials make it easier for the good teacher to do what *could* be done with poorer materials; improvements increase the mileage teachers get from equal expenditures of time and energy.

There are three major categories of materials to be considered: (1) materials intended specifically for the teaching of reading, (2) library materials, and (3) content area materials. There have never been so many new materials in each of these categories as have flowed from the publishers in the last two or three years. Two major developments have changed the complexion of many of these materials. The first is the strong emphasis on relevance for today's children and youth. Many teachers feel that difficulty of materials, to which so much attention has been paid in the past, is less important than this relevance. In fact, some feel the lack of relevance may be a major cause of the difficulty. The second trend is toward a multimedia approach.

Relevance is very difficult, if not impossible, to define briefly. We usually think of it as related to interests: a story, for example, is relevant to a group of students if it deals with situations or ideas which they perceive as meaningful and important to them. However, in another sense, materials are relevant if they are expressed in a language which coincides with the language which is familiar to the readers. There has been much discussion of late of the irrelevance, in this sense, of the language of many basal readers. The rationale for the use of the experience approach to early reading depends in part on this matter of relevance of language. Good experience charts are expressed in the actual dialect of the pupils who create and use them.

What is relevant in one situation may very well not be in another. Hence, the great variety of materials now appearing: those for "urban" pupils, for the "turned-off," for the "children without." In the struggle to find or create materials which have immediate and obvious relevance, it would sometimes appear that teachers have given up trying to *make* books relevant to youngsters. Effective teaching can show the students the ways in which experiences and ideas they have not personally or immediately encountered may, very probably, have something important to say to them if they will but make a little effort to listen. Great literature *is* great literature precisely because it deals with basic human issues and emotions. Alienated youngsters need desperately to sense that they belong to mankind, and we should not throw away too easily the books which have best expressed these ideas. Teachers can be too quick to accept materials dealing, for example, with violence and brutality because they believe that these are what students want, forgetting, perhaps, that themes of courage, honor, pride, hope, compassion are also relevant, though perhaps less obviously so.

It may, indeed, be a fact that the teacher of some turned-off groups cannot even get started unless he uses materials which immediately appeal to their sense of the timely and the important. It must be recognized, of course, that some of these materials which have immediate relevance also have great literary merit. Others are obviously shoddy, written to sell to a market which has suddenly become very much concerned about the timeliness of instructional content. Curriculum committees and individual teachers must evaluate more carefully than they have ever needed to do before. Hopefully, they will not discard all the fine materials which have served well in the past. If they do not succeed in persuading young people that these books, too, are relevant because they deal with great universal themes, they will probably have had little real influence on the students' understanding of literature.

The multimedia trend has mushroomed. We are now at the transition stage between the use of media other than books as only adjuncts to instruction and the acceptance of such media as central in the teaching process. Many psychologists insist that learning takes place most rapidly if as many senses as possible are used in the process; teachers are looking for variety to capture the attention of students; moreover, we live in an era of the "packaged deal." These influences, together with increasing sophistication in electronic devices, have led to the presenting of educational materials in packages: packages of books or cards at first, but now packages of books and filmstrips, and records, and tapes, and transparencies, and filmloops, materials of all kinds and in all kinds of combinations. Some of these packages make very good educational sense while others have obviously been put together hurriedly and shoddily in an effort to capitalize on a trend.

Teachers and others charged with selection of materials have a whole new problem in the evaluation of this kind of material.

Publishers obviously can make very few samples available because of the cost of the components of these packages. Large school systems can usually arrange to have sets of the materials left for a few days for evaluation—a very time-consuming process if done thoroughly. Smaller school systems seldom have a chance for thorough evaluation. There is a real need for groups of school systems and/or state departments of education to provide centers, mobile if possible, where teachers and others can go to see and evaluate such multimedia materials before investing what may amount to thousands of dollars. It is a very different problem from that posed by a decision involving a trial set of textbooks.

There are, of course, a few very basic considerations applicable to materials in any of the three major categories: Will the format be attractive to children? Is the material relevant in more than a superficial sense to *these* children at *this* time? Will it serve some clearly identified purpose better than something else which might be chosen?

Materials for Teaching Reading Skills

Questions become much more specific when we look at each category separately. When we are considering what materials we should assemble to carry on the actual teaching of reading, we need to seek out the answers to these questions:

1. Do we have materials with which we can carry on a strong prereading program with major emphasis on the development of oral-aural skills?
2. Do the materials reflect the best that is known about the application of linguistic science?
3. Do they provide the means by which a strong study skills program can be built?
4. Do the teachers' editions of manuals provide rich, well-organized, but readily adaptable suggestions for implementing the materials?
5. Do the materials provide enough variety so that students can be taught to read fact, fiction, poetry, drama?
6. Will the materials help or hinder efforts to individualize instruction?

7. Are accompanying study questions geared *in the main* to interpretation, to critical and creative thinking, rather than to factual recall? This criterion alone will rule out most of the shoddy, hastily constructed material.
8. What provision is made within the material itself for continuing diagnosis of skills? If we believe that diagnostic teaching is imperative, we must supply teachers with the means to do it.
9. If the material is of the more costly types (as compared with books and workbooks) is it really worth the price because it can accomplish the purpose better?

It is not possible to set up any absolute guidelines for choosing these materials. In Community A, for example, there may be relatively little need for a strong oral-aural readiness program because most children come from cultivated, highly verbal homes and have, by the age of five or six, already stowed thousands of words into their speaking-listening vocabularies. In Community B, on the other hand, kindergarten children may not even be able to name pictures of everyday things like a lawnmower or a sidewalk.

Library Materials

We should apply specific criteria such as these when choosing library materials:

Do the materials support and enrich the curriculum and thus encourage teachers to move from a limited textbook approach to richer possibilities?

Are they in tune with what is known about the interests of children and young adults?

Are they up-to-date? In some areas, like science, this criterion may be crucial.

Do they contribute to a well-balanced, comprehensive library collection?

Is there a good balance among the various media? Do the materials other than books coordinate well with the book collection?

Content Area Materials

Content area materials make up the third major category. Until recently, these materials have been evaluated mainly in terms of *what facts* they contained rather than in terms of readability or of the contribution they can make to developing students' ability to study effectively and independently. Now we are beginning to ask this kind of question about these content materials:

How readable are they for the students with whom we intend to use them?

What devices are included which will help the student grow in ability to study as well as in knowledge of content?

What devices are used to help the teacher teach study skills at the same time that he is teaching content?

Publishers of all kinds of materials are very sensitive to teacher readiness to accept new kinds of materials. Better materials come when enough teachers have indicated often enough that they are ready. Market research is just good business practice. Major publishers are deeply responsible professionally, but the impetus for change does not usually originate with them. They listen and watch and try to give teachers what they will use.

The Reading Program Itself

When is a reading program successful? The more hard headed teacher and administrator wants real objective proof that students are reading better and more than they have done in the past. These facts are not easy to come by.

On the theoretical level, there is considerable agreement about what a sound reading program should be like. Generally speaking, we ought to be able to say the following things:

It is a well-rounded program giving attention not only to both basic and specialized skills and their application in all appropriate ways but also to the affective aspects of the process.

It is a respecter of all groups of students: the handicapped, the gifted, the ethnically or socially different.

It is also a respecter of individuals and provides for their needs and interests so far as it is possible to do so.

It is continuous and sequential through the entire range of a school system's responsibility.

It is as relevant as possible to conditions in a school and a community.

It is implemented by the entire professional staff, which keeps up with the best available theory and practice.

It exists in an atmosphere of expected success on the part of both teachers and students.

It is supported by a community which willingly supplies the funds for adequate staffing and materials.

It is continuously evaluated and changed if evaluation indicates that change is required.

Results of the Program

There is no easy way to measure the actual results of so complex an effort as a school reading program. Some of the attempts to do so are distressingly naive. What we really need to know is both how well students *can* perform and how well they *do* perform.

More often than not, the chief criterion is some kind of standardized testing program. This is a questionable procedure for two reasons.

The normative data supplied with these tests must be interpreted in local terms, and such interpretation is largely subjective and fraught with opportunity for bias. National norms are particularly dangerous in schools with a high percentage of disadvantaged students. If results of testing are compared to such norms and revealed to students and their parents, they can only hurt the pride and depress the motivation of such students. They may also hurt the pride and depress the motivation of the teachers who, though more knowledgeable about such things, often respond with a what's-the-use attitude. What students, parents, and teachers all need to know is how the results of an individual student's tests compare with those of his peers in the same setting.

Norms always represent what the pupils who were used in the standardization process actually were producing, not what they *could* produce under better conditions. Hence, the strong tendency to think of such norms as goals to be attained encourages satisfaction with less than the potentially best.

Yet, if standardized tests are not used, what possibilities for completely objective evaluation are there? The discouraging answer to this question has forced many persons to use standardized tests, hoping they are wise enough to interpret the results reasonably well, rather than forego objective evaluation almost completely. Are there any other criteria for measuring the end product which are at least semi-objective?

It is certainly possible for an individual teacher, a school, or a school system to build semi-objective criteria for evaluating each of the behavioral objectives described on page 49. No comparisons with an independent criterion can be made, but at least teachers can have evidence that they have, or have not, achieved certain specific goals developed and accepted locally.

Appraisal of attitude about reading is especially difficult. Perhaps one measure of this is to be found in such statistics as library circulation and sale of books and other printed materials. Such statistics, too, have to be interpreted with care. While library circulation is increasing, so is the population, and while there is some indication that a few people are reading more than in the past, most people are not reading at all, at least not books.

What of Tomorrow?

The future encroaches on the present so rapidly that there never seems to be any time to get ready for it. In an increasingly technological society with its concomitantly increased tensions and greater amounts of leisure time for almost everyone, the years ahead demand not only that literacy levels be raised but also that reading become one means of better individual life adjustment. It may well be that in the almost immediate future some of the reading skills—for example, "how to read a card catalogue"—will become obsolete; computers will probably take over such jobs. It may be, too, that more "reading" will be done with the ear instead of the eye for we may soon be able to pick up a telephone, ask a question, and hear the answer from a data resource center. But essentially there is little difference, as has been pointed out earlier, between the processes of reading and of listening.

As teachers, we can undoubtedly anticipate many changes in all aspects of the reading program discussed in this monograph. Changes, creatively used, can mean better reading for many pupils. Better understanding of children and more attractive and varied physical surroundings could create a better climate for learning. Better organizational structure and improved materials should make classroom teaching more relevant and personal—a closer approximation of individual instruction. Teachers can know more success in their work if their need to continue to learn is satisfied through rewarding inservice experiences. Finally, if the reading curriculum is constructed in clear and precise terms, no one can mistake its objectives. Given these conditions, reading programs in the schools will have a better chance to produce a sound foundation on which to build children's further education.